HISPANIC AMERICA

1990s to 2010

BY
STEVEN OTFINOSKI

Marshall Cavendish
Benchmark
New York

Thanks to José Guevara-Escudero, Ph.D., CFP, professor of Latin American Studies in the History department at Pace University, for his expert reading of this manuscript.

MARSHALL CAVENDISH BENCHMARK
99 WHITE PLAINS ROAD
TARRYTOWN, NEW YORK 10591-5502
www.marshallcavendish.us

Text copyright © 2009 by Marshall Cavendish Corporation

All rights reserved. No part of this book may be reproduced or utilized in any form or by any means electronic or mechanical, including photocopying, recording, or by any information storage and retrieval system, without permission from the copyright holders.

All websites were available and accurate when this book was sent to press.

LIBRARY OF CONGRESS CATALOGING-IN-PUBLICATION DATA
Otfinoski, Steven.
1990-2010 / by Steven Otfinoski.
p. cm. — (Hispanic America)
Includes bibliographical references and index.
Summary: "Provides comprehensive information on the history of the Spanish coming to the United States, focusing on the decades of the 1990s to 2010"—Provided by publisher.
ISBN 978-0-7614-4180-9
1. Hispanic Americans—History—20th century—Juvenile literature. 2. Hispanic Americans—History—21st century—Juvenile literature. 3. Hispanic Americans—Social conditions—20th century—Juvenile literature. 4. Hispanic Americans—Social conditions—21st century—Juvenile literature. 5. United States—Race relations—History—20th century—Juvenile literature. 6. United States—Race relations—History—21st century—Juvenile literature. 7. United States—Emigration and immigration—History—20th century—Juvenile literature. 8. United States—Emigration and immigration—History—21st century—Juvenile literature. 9. Latin America—Emigration and immigration—History—20th century—Juvenile literature. 10. Latin America—Emigration and immigration—History—21st century—Juvenile literature. I. Title. II. Title: Nineteen ninety-two thousand ten.
E184.S75.O838 2009
305.800973—dc22
2008043962

Photo research by Tracey Engel

Cover: Getty Images/David McNew
Title page: Getty Images/ADALBERTO ROQUE/AFP
Back cover: Alamy/JUPITERIMAGES/ Comstock Images
The photographs in this book are used by permission and through the courtesy of:
Alamy: David Young-Wolff, 4; Jeff Greenberg, 21; Ambient Images Inc., 29; Richard Levine, 30; Jeff Greenberg, 32; JUPITERIMAGES/Comstock Images, 63. *AP Images*: Paul Sakuma, 13; John Hayes, 35; Matt York, 37; Alan Diaz, 44, 46; Francis Specker, 48. *Corbis*: Tannen Maury/epa, 10; Karen Kasmauski, 12; Nik Wheeler, 18; Patrick Ward, 20; Stephanie Maze, 24; Ted Soqui, 26; Bob E. Daemmrich/Sygma, 40; REUTERS/Colin Braley, 50; Aristide Economopoulos/Star Ledger, 57; Rick Gomez, 60; LARRY DOWNING/Reuters, 67; Brooks Kraft, 68. *Getty Images*: David McNew, 8; Warren K. Leffler, Library of Congress - digital version copyright Science Faction, 16; Alexander Tamargo, 22; Mark Wilson, 31; Sandy Huffaker, 39; DOUG COLLIER/AFP, 42; Jon Kopaloff/FilmMagic, 53; Randy Brooke/WireImage, 54; Baerbel Schmidt, 58; ADALBERTO ROQUE/AFP, 71.

EDITOR: Joy Bean   PUBLISHER: Michelle Bisson
ART DIRECTOR: Anahid Hamparian   SERIES DESIGNER: Kristen Branch

Printed in Malaysia
1 3 5 6 4 2

Contents

CHAPTER ONE
The Hispanic Explosion 5

CHAPTER TWO
The Big Three 19

CHAPTER THREE
The Immigration Question 33

CHAPTER FOUR
A Changing Culture 49

CHAPTER FIVE
Looking to the Future 61

Glossary 74
Further Information 76
Bibliography 77
Index 78

CHAPTER ONE

The Hispanic Explosion

JANUARY 22, 2003 WAS AN IMPORTANT DAY IN Hispanic American history and American history as well. That day the U.S. Census Bureau made a startling announcement. According to the bureau's latest population figures, Hispanics had become the largest minority group in the United States, totaling 37 million. For the first time, Hispanics had surpassed African Americans, who totaled 36.2 million. Although the difference in numbers between the two groups was not great, in the years since 2003, Hispanics have widened the gap. This is due to two things. One, Hispanics have a higher birth rate than any other ethnic or racial group. Two, Hispanic *immigration* has escalated rapidly.

Five years later, in 2008, the Hispanic population had risen to more than 45 million, making up 15.1 percent of the total

Opposite: Hispanics make up a large part of the U.S. population.

5

population of the United States. By 2020, some experts believe, Hispanics will make up 20 percent of the U.S. population. They predict that at current growth rates, one in three Americans will be Hispanic by 2100.

So what exactly is a Hispanic American? The term includes all American residents or citizens whose ancestors come from Spain or a Spanish-speaking country. Most Hispanic Americans come from Latin America—Mexico, the islands of the West Indies, Central America, and South America. In some of these countries, Portuguese or French is the primary language.

In the early 1500s, Spanish and Portuguese explorers and settlers began to arrive in the Americas. In the lands south of the present-day United States, some of these Europeans intermarried with Native Americans, as well as Africans initially brought to the Americas as slaves. Today, most Hispanics living in Latin America are of mixed ancestry. The remainder of the population belongs to one of these three races—white, Native American, or black.

FROM MAINE TO CALIFORNIA

Where do all these Hispanic Americans live? About half of them are concentrated in three states—Texas, California, and New York. Other states that have large numbers of Hispanics are Florida, Illinois, Arizona, New Jersey, Colorado, New Mexico, and Georgia. Hispanics—who can be any race—outnumber non-Hispanic whites (also called *Anglos*) in Los

Opposite: Latin America is made up of Mexico and the countries in Central and South America.

Angeles, California, and in the Texas metropolises of Houston, San Antonio, and Dallas. The current Hispanic population of Illinois is expected to nearly double by 2020, thus making Hispanics the state's largest minority group.

But Hispanics do not live only in big states and big cities. They can be found in communities of every size in every state of the Union. Portland, Maine, has 115,000 Hispanic residents and Anchorage, Alaska, has 18,000. A 2005 survey showed that the Hispanic population was growing faster in the *suburbs* of New York City than in the city itself. The flight of Hispanics from the city is economically driven. The suburbs now offer more job opportunities and cheaper housing for Hispanics than New York City does.

In a ceremony held in March 2000, 8,165 immigrants were sworn in as U.S. citizens. 5,311 of those immigrants were from Mexico.

Rural areas are also seeing an influx of Hispanics. In 2006, more than 114,000 Hispanics were living in Iowa. In some of this state's smallest towns, about one-third of the population is Hispanic. Walking down the main streets of small towns in the American heartland, you are likely to see Mexican restaurants, Cuban grocery stores, and newsstands selling Spanish-language newspapers and magazines.

A Sleeping Giant Awakens

For decades, the Hispanic population of the United States has been an invisible and forgotten minority for many people. In many cities, Hispanics kept to themselves in their own neighborhoods, spoke Spanish, and had little interaction with other Americans. This isolation partly resulted from discrimination. Some Anglos looked down on Hispanics and viewed them as uneducated, poor, and suspicious foreigners who refused to learn English. Hispanics generally were considered only for unskilled, manual-labor jobs, such as gardening and housecleaning. Some African Americans were prejudiced toward Hispanics. They saw Hispanics as taking away limited job opportunities.

In the last twenty years, life has begun to change for Hispanics in the United States. Children of Hispanic parents—many of them immigrants—speak English, go to college, and have successful careers. Many have discovered the power of the ballot and they are voting for politicians who address their concerns. Hispanics have played a major

New Mexico's first Hispanic governor, Bill Richardson, ran in the presidential primaries in 2008.

role in the past several presidential elections, and their influence will continue to grow. Bill Richardson, who was elected the first Hispanic governor of New Mexico in 2002, ran in the Democratic presidential primaries of 2008.

Economically, Hispanic buying power is huge. Hispanic Americans have had a major influence in entertainment, food, and fashion. In 2008, the Hispanic consumer market generated more than $860 billion in sales in the United States. Hispanic-owned and operated radio and television stations draw millions of listeners and viewers. Latin American foods are popular with many Americans, both in restaurants and on the family dinner table. Many of these foods were brought over from native lands by immigrants who sold them to their country people in restaurants and small stores. These businesses remain some of the first and best economic activities for immigrants. Over time, non-Hispanic Americans discovered these foods and grew to love them. In fact, a few years ago the sale of *salsa* surpassed that of ketchup. The Hispanic explosion is being felt across the nation.

Mexican Americans

Who are the Hispanics that are changing the face of America? Many are immigrants from more than two dozen countries in Latin America. The largest group is Mexican Americans, who numbered more than 28 million in 2006. The great majority of Mexican Americans live in the West and the Southwest, where some Mexican Americans have been living for hundreds of years. Large Mexican American populations can also be found in the Midwest and the Southeast. Many Mexican Americans left Mexico to find better jobs and living conditions in the United States.

Many Mexican Americans have entered the United States legally, but many others have not. Some *undocumented immigrants* cross the long U.S.-Mexico border by swimming the Rio Grande, a river along the Texas border, or by traveling across the desert on foot or in vehicles. These people risk their lives to come to the United States. Some die from drowning or of dehydration along the way. Others are caught by immigration police and are sent home—perhaps to try again another time.

A young Mexican boy scales the fence separating the United States and Mexico near Tijuana.

Many undocumented Mexican American immigrants are farmers and unskilled laborers. Even people who had a better-paying profession in Mexico are often forced to find different types of work because they are not certified to perform their professions in the United States.

Mexican Americans, like other Hispanics, are proud of their heritage. They keep it alive in their traditions, their festivals, and their day-to-day lives.

Puerto Rican Americans

In 2003, Puerto Rican Americans—also called Stateside Puerto Ricans—experienced their own landmark statistics.

Mexicans are proud of their heritage, and proud of being Americans.

For the first time, Puerto Ricans living on the mainland United States outnumbered their compatriots living in Puerto Rico. About four million Puerto Ricans lived in each region, with those on the mainland edging out the island residents by about 163,000. It was the first time in history that emigrants had outnumbered native residents in any country in the Western Hemisphere.

Two reasons for this vast migration are the poverty and lack of job opportunities in Puerto Rico. Another reason is the ease with which Puerto Ricans can move to the United States. As a *commonwealth* of the United States since 1917, Puerto Rico holds a special status among Latin American countries.

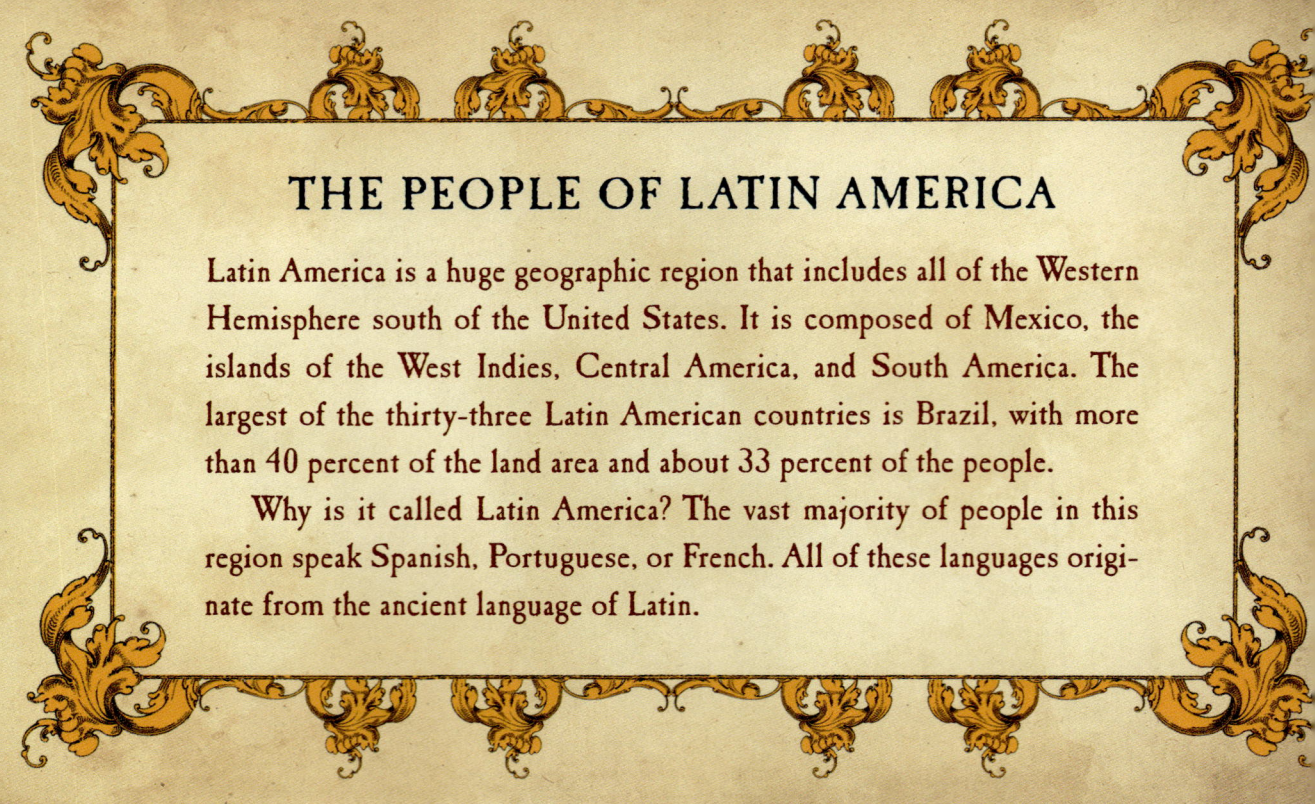

Its residents are American citizens and do not need a special *visa* to come and live on the mainland. However, they do not have the right to vote in presidential elections unless they are living in the continental United States.

Puerto Ricans form the second-largest group of Hispanics in America. Traditionally, Puerto Rican Americans have settled in large urban centers in the Northeast and the Midwest. But in recent years Puerto Ricans have been growing in numbers in other states, particularly Florida. The states with the largest Puerto Rican populations are New York, Florida, New Jersey, Pennsylvania, and Massachusetts.

Cuban Americans

Unlike Mexican and Puerto Rican immigrants, most Cuban Americans moved to America in search of political freedom as much as economic opportunity. About 1.5 million Cubans have fled their homeland since *communist* dictator Fidel Castro came to power in 1959. Many thousands died while attempting to cross the 90 miles (145 kilometers) of ocean that separates Cuba from the United States.

In August 1994, Cuba experienced the largest antigovernment rally in the history of Castro's regime. Government troops crushed the demonstration, but shortly afterward Castro agreed to allow protesters who sought to leave Cuba to do so. By mid-September, 32,000 Cubans had crossed to the United States in boats and rafts. It was the largest exodus of Cubans from their homeland in fourteen years. In 1980, after the Cuban economy took a sharp downturn, a large number of Cubans departed from Cuba's Mariel Harbor for the United States. This was called the Mariel Boatlift.

The 2000 U.S. Census counted more than 1.2 million Cuban Americans, making them the third-largest Hispanic American group from a single country. Most Cuban Americans live in Florida, New York, New Jersey, California, and Illinois. Because many were political exiles of some wealth, Cuban Americans in general are better educated, have a higher percentage of professional and white-collar workers, and enjoy higher incomes than other

Cuban leader Fidel Castro's harsh rule has caused more than a million Cubans to leave their homeland.

1990s to 2010

16

Hispanic Americans do. Because of their intense feelings against Castro and communism, many Cuban Americans are more politically conservative than other Hispanics. They are proud patriots of their new homeland, and many support the Republican Party, which has traditionally been strongly anticommunist.

OTHER HISPANIC AMERICANS

Mexicans, Puerto Ricans, and Cubans make up about three-quarters of the Hispanic population of the United States. The remaining quarter is composed of immigrants from many other Latin American countries. Large groups from single Latin American countries come from the Dominican Republic and El Salvador (about 3 percent each). About 5 percent are from South American countries, and 4 percent come from the other nations of Central America. Some of these immigrants fled from devastating civil wars in countries such as Guatemala and Nicaragua. About 8 percent of the remaining Hispanics come from Spain, Caribbean islands, and other Hispanic countries outside of Latin America.

CHAPTER TWO

The Big Three

WHILE HISPANIC AMERICANS ARE HAVING A tremendous impact on American society, that impact is perhaps most dramatic in three of the country's largest metropolises: Miami, Florida; Los Angeles, California; and New York City, New York. While one nationality dominates Hispanic life in each city, many other Hispanic peoples enrich the life and culture of these great metropolises.

Little Havana

Arguably, no urban center in the United States is more Hispanic than Miami. Outside of Latin America, no single city has as large a Spanish-speaking population. Of the city's more than 386,000 people, only about a quarter speak English. Miami-Dade County, of which Miami is the county seat (the center of

Opposite: Cuban dancers celebrate their culture during the Carnaval Miami, a two-week-long festival of Cuban culture.

government for the county), is home to more than 650,000 Cuban Americans. Some Cuban Americans have been there for generations. Many others belong to the "Golden Exile" generation of the early 1960s, which fled Cuba after the 1959 revolution that put Fidel Castro in power. Others came in subsequent waves of exiles that to this day continue to bring Cubans to the United States. Many stayed in southern Florida, their point of entry, a region with a geography and climate similar to that of their homeland.

Little Havana, home to many of Miami's Cubans, stretches from Twelfth Avenue to Twenty-seventh Avenue in the southwestern district of the city. No part of the city more brilliantly reflects Cuban life and culture. You can shop in the many open-air markets, listen to rhythmic

Cuban men play chess and smoke cigars in a park in Little Havana.

Cuban music played on guitar or by a band, or sit at a sidewalk café with a cup of *cafecito*, strong Cuban coffee topped with a sugar foam called *espumita*.

Little Havana is especially exciting during the two-week long Carnaval Miami festival in early March. There are colorful parades, dazzling fireworks displays, live outdoor concerts, and plenty of good Cuban food to eat. The festival reaches its climax at the Calle Ocho Open House, when more than a million people crowd into a twenty-three-block area along Eighth Street to party, to eat, and to listen to music.

Cubans are not the only Hispanics who call Miami home. There is the neighborhood of Little Haiti, home to a large Haitian American population. Haitian *Creole* is one of the city's three official languages, along with English and Spanish.

A Haitian living in Miami volunteers her time to keep her neighborhood clean.

THE BIG THREE

Other neighborhoods include Little Brazil; Little San Juan, home to Miami's Puerto Ricans; and Little Managua, named for the capital of Nicaragua, homeland of the second-largest Hispanic group in Miami. There are also sizable communities of Hondurans, Dominicans, and Colombians, as well as immigrants from a number of other South American countries and Caribbean islands.

Telemundo soap opera stars Miguel Varoni (l.) and Sebastian Ligarde pose during a viewing party, held in Miami, for their show *Pecados Ajenos*.

In the book *South America's Immigrants to the United States: The Flight from Turmoil*, D. H. Figueredo wrote, "You can shop at a supermarket owned by Cubans, visit an Uruguayan doctor, buy medicines from a pharmacy owned by a Chilean, and socialize at restaurants with folks from the Dominican Republic. You can vote for a Spanish-speaking official and listen to the news in Spanish. You can go for days without hearing English spoken."

Miami is a major center for Hispanic television and film production. Spanish-language game shows and variety shows are filmed in Miami studios. So are the popular Hispanic soap operas called *telenovelas*, although the production is controlled by television companies in Latin countries such as Mexico and Argentina.

1990s to 2010

While Cuban Americans in Miami have close ties to relatives and friends back in Cuba, most of them are anti-Castro, strongly anticommunist, and Republicans. Former Republican president Ronald Reagan is a hero to many Cuban Americans for his strong stand against Castro and communism. There is a major turnpike in Miami named in Reagan's honor.

Southern Florida has many Cuban American office holders and government officials in southern Florida. On the state level, Mel Martinez, who served as secretary of housing and urban development (HUD) under President George W. Bush, was elected as a U.S. senator from Florida in 2004. Martinez, a Republican, is the first Cuban American to serve in the Senate. In 2006, Republican Marco Rubio, also Cuban, was elected by his colleagues as speaker of the Florida House of Representatives, an office he held until November 2008.

City of the Angels

In 2000, California became only the second mainland state (after New Mexico) to be a "majority-minority" society. That year the white non-Hispanic population became a minority for the first time since 1848, as nearly 47 percent of the population was Hispanic. Los Angeles County was two years ahead of the state, however. In 1998, Hispanics had outnumbered non-Hispanic whites by more than a million.

A wall painting on a housing project in Boyle Heights in Los Angeles shows Che Guevara saying "We are not a minority."

The Hispanic population of Los Angeles is large and diverse. There are 133,000 residents of South American origin—the third-largest number of South Americans in any U.S. city. Central Americans are also well represented. Los Angeles has more Salvadorans than El Salvador's capital, San Salvadore. But by far the most dominant Hispanic group in the city is Mexican Americans. They are mostly concentrated in East Los Angeles, a community that is home to more than 120,000 *first-generation* and *second-generation* Hispanic immigrants.

East L.A. is not without its problems. For decades it has been plagued by crime and poverty. Thousands of young

Mexican Americans belong to gangs that commit crimes and fight with other gangs for territory on the streets. Some of the most violent fighting happens between Mexican American and African American gangs. For a decade and a half, the Mexican Mafia and the Black Guerilla Family—gangs made up of former prison inmates—have been killing each other for control of the region's drug trade.

Since he became mayor of Los Angeles in 2005, Mexican American Antonio Villaraigosa (see sidebar, pages 26–27) has been working hard to break up the gangs, reduce violence, and improve schools. He has only been partially successful. In 2006, gang violence increased by 14 percent. By 2008, however, a significant drop in crime in gang neighborhoods took place.

There is other positive news in East L.A. In 2007, an Anglo doctor named Robert Krochmal helped start a community garden in a half-acre vacant lot. Proyecto Jardín (Project Garden) has become a symbol of community pride in the neighborhood. It is supplementing the unhealthy, fast-food diets of many Hispanic children with fresh vegetables and fruits that they and their families are growing themselves. Hundreds of residents participate in harvest celebrations at the garden.

Los Angeles has recently surpassed Miami and New York City as the biggest hub of Hispanic television production. In 2007, the cable network LATV, the first *bilingual* music and entertainment cable network in the United

ANTONIO VILLARAIGOSA, AN HISPANIC MAYOR FOR ALL LOS ANGELANS

In May 2005, Mexican American Antonio Villaraigosa became the first Hispanic mayor of Los Angeles in 133 years. He won the mayor's office by putting together a political coalition of Hispanic, Anglo, and black voters.

Villaraigosa was born Antonio Villar in a poor family into East L.A. on January 23, 1953. His parents divorced when he was five, and he was raised by his mother, a part-time secretary. In tenth grade, he was diagnosed with a tumor in his spine that paralyzed him from the waist down. He eventually recovered.

Villar got expelled from high school after participating in a fight at a school football game. Herman Katz, an English teacher at another high school Villar attended, took an interest in him and became his mentor. With Katz's support, Villar went on to the University of California at Los Angeles (UCLA) and graduated in 1977. He later married Corina Raigosa, and they combined their last names. Villaraigosa became the field representative for United Teachers of Los Angeles (UTLA) and president of the Los Angeles chapter of the American Civil Liberties Union (ACLU). In 1994, Villaraigosa won his first election to the California State Assembly. Four years later, his colleagues voted him assembly speaker. He was the first Hispanic in twenty-five years to serve in that position.

As mayor, Villaraigosa has worked hard to improve Los Angeles. He repaired roadways that eased the flow of L.A.'s heavy traffic. He has supported the Clean Air Ports Act Plan to improve air quality, helped the city's thousands of homeless people, and initiated a program to plant one million new trees in Los Angeles. This ambitious Democratic politician may one day run for governor or U.S. senator of his state.

States, went national with digital satellite broadcasting. In 2008, Telemundo, the nation's second-largest producer of Spanish content in the world, opened a new 16,000-square-foot production studio complex. The city is also home to the largest Spanish-speaking television network, Univision network.

The Nuyoricans

New York City is the most highly populated city in the nation, and Puerto Ricans have been its largest Hispanic minority for decades. During the "Great Migration" (1946–1964), about two-fifths of the population of Puerto Rico immigrated to New York and other eastern coast cities searching to find a better life. Most of the immigrants found steady jobs in manufacturing, but by the 1980s, many factories had closed or had moved to other parts of the country where they could operate more cheaply.

These immigrants have come to be called Nuyoricans, a blending of "New York" and "Puerto Rican." This term dates back at least to 1975, when a group of Puerto Rican writers began to congregate at the Nuyorican Poets Café. These writers took pride in the name, but Nuyorican became a derogatory term used by native Puerto Ricans, who viewed Nuyoricans as uncultured. More recently, the term has lost some of its negativity as more and more Puerto Ricans have traveled to the United States and Nuyoricans have moved to other states.

A restaurant in East Harlem is visited by the many Puerto Ricans living in the area.

THE BIG THREE

THE PUERTO RICAN DAY PARADE

Puerto Rican labor leader Dennis Rivera has called the National Puerto Rican Day Parade "the largest parade probably in the universe." That might be a slight exaggeration, but this parade is one of the biggest events in the life of this teeming city. It attracts more than 80,000 participants and about two million spectators.

The fifty-first parade was held on June 8, 2008, with Rivera serving as its grand marshall. Previous parade leaders have included Puerto Rican singers Marc Anthony and Ricky Martin. The parade route passes up Fifth Avenue from Forty-fourth to Eighty-sixth Streets. It includes colorful floats, marching bands, entertainers and musicians.

For weeks before the parade, the Puerto Rican community holds dozens of cultural and social events, culminating in the 116th Street Festival, which is held the day before. More than fifty smaller parades honoring Puerto Ricans are held throughout the United States on the same day.

Today, New York remains the main destination for new Puerto Rican immigrants, although many do not stay. East Harlem (also known as *El Barrio*), on Manhattan's Upper East Side, and Washington Heights are the two main communities of New York's Puerto Ricans.

While poverty remains a major problem for Nuyoricans, their long involvement in community action and politics has provided hope and support. In 1992, Brooklyn Democrat Nydia Velazquez, the daughter of a sugarcane worker in Puerto Rico, became the first Puerto Rican woman elected to the U.S. House of Representatives as a representative of Brooklyn, one of New York City's five boroughs. As of 2008, she was serving her eighth term in Congress.

Nydia Velazquez was the first Puerto Rican woman elected to the House of Representatives.

New York City is also home to the largest community of Dominicans in the United States and the largest urban population of South American residents.

CHAPTER THREE

The Immigration Question

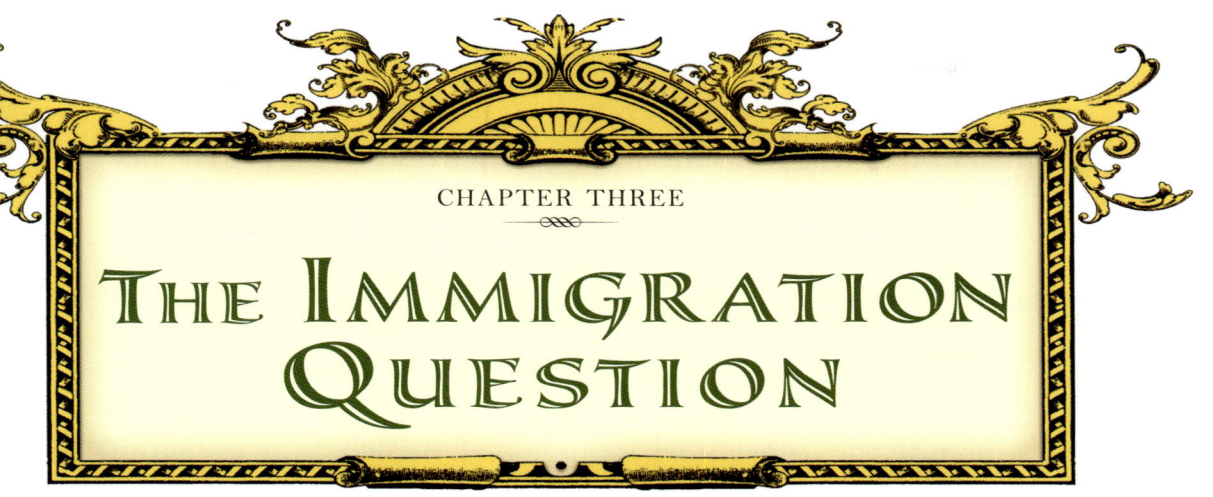

MAY DAY 2006, TRADITIONALLY A DAY TO honor workers, was a landmark in the history of labor protests in the United States. Across the nation, millions of workers, most of them Hispanic Americans, walked off their jobs, and caused many businesses to shut down. Thousands of Hispanic high school students left their classrooms. It was a culmination of more than a month of demonstrations and protests against the Border Protection, Anti-terrorism and Illegal Immigration Control Act of 2005. This bill was passed in the House of Representatives on December 16, 2005 by a vote of 239 to 182. Among other measures, the law would make illegal entry by immigrants a *felony*. Assisting illegal immigrants would also become a punishable crime.

Opposite: Immigrants across the country went on strike in May 2006 to protest against a number of acts the House of Representatives had passed that limited the actions of immigrants.

Many of the protestors were illegal immigrants. Those who were not had relatives or friends who were. Even legal Hispanic immigrants felt that too many Americans saw all Hispanic Americans as "illegals." They predicted that the new law, if passed, would have a negative effect on all Hispanic Americans' lives. The massive protest also demonstrated how much the American economy depended on the labor of illegal immigrants. In the end, it helped lead to the failure of the legislation in the U.S. Senate. The Senate passed its own modified immigration bill on May 25, 2006, but it failed to pass a conference committee, a committee of Congress appointed to resolve disagreements on a bill. Neither bill has been resubmitted since then.

"We're all very aware that this is history in the making, and the country will be transformed by it," declared Cecila Muñoz, vice president for policy with the National Council of La Raza, a Hispanics rights organization.

A National Debate

Illegal immigration—particularly from Mexico and Central America—has been a hot topic for decades. By the early 1980s, even committed liberals such as California Senator Alan Simpson were questioning whether the United States could keep its doors open to the millions of Hispanic immigrants pouring across the U.S.-Mexico border. "We have to live within limits," said Simpson in 1982. "The nation wants to be compassionate but we have been compassionate beyond our ability to respond."

The issue came into the national spotlight once again in the early 1990s. Two of President Bill Clinton's cabinet nominees, including attorney general nominee Zoe Baird, were forced to withdraw from nomination when it was discovered that they had hired illegal Hispanic workers to help with their households. The matter of illegal immigration came to a head in August 1993 when California governor Pete Wilson proposed a constitutional amendment that would deny citizenship to all children of illegal immigrants—even though the children were born in the United States. Under present law, all children gain automatic citizenship if they are born inside the country. The proposal did not pass.

California governor Pete Wilson upset many people when he asked the government to deny citizenship to all children of illegal immigrants born in the United States.

Immigration became a concern again in 2001. The terrorist attacks on New York City and Washington, D.C., on September 11 heightened concern about the safety and security of U.S. borders—particularly the 2,000-mile (3,219-km) border between Mexico and the United States.

As the 2008 presidential election approached, political arguments for and against tolerance of illegal immigrants grew more vocal. In a survey taken in June 2007, 63 percent of

THE IMMIGRATION QUESTION
35

Americans who participated said they would support an immigration policy that allows illegal immigrants to become citizens if they "pass background checks, pay fines and have jobs."

The immigration issue is not as clear-cut as people on both sides sometimes make it. It is impossible to determine how the flow of illegal immigrants will affect the U.S. economy *infrastructure* in the years to come. Legal Hispanic and other immigrants have not been able to fill all the jobs necessary for the service-driven economy, and many American-born workers do not want these relatively low-paying jobs. Even if they did, the low native-born birthrate has created a gap in the workforce that illegal workers have been able to fill. Many employers, particularly in the west, have welcomed illegal immigrants because their businesses could not survive without this source of labor.

Sealing Off the Border

In 2006, Congress authorized the U.S. Department of Homeland Security to construct 700 miles (1,127 km) of fencing along the U.S.-Mexico border from Brownsville, Texas, to California. The department's goal was to complete 670 miles (1,078 km) of the fencing by the end of 2008, but only half of that amount was completed on time. Given the controversy surrounding "the wall," as many locals call the 50-foot-high (15-meter-high) fence, it was no surprise that the deadline was not met.

National Guardsmen weld a section of the wall separating Mexico from Arizona in an effort to keep illegal immigrants from crossing into the United States.

THE IMMIGRATION QUESTION

Property owners along the border disapprove of the wall that splits up their land. Many politicians, both for and against illegal immigration, believe the wall will make little difference in the flow of immigrants. "You show me a 50-foot wall and I'll show you a 51-foot ladder at the border," said Arizona governor Janet Napolitano, whose state has an estimated 500,000 illegal immigrants.

In May 2008, the Texas Border Coalition—an organization of local politicians, commissioners, and economists—filed a federal lawsuit against the U.S. Department of Homeland Security in an effort to halt the fence construction. The coalition, along with many other critics, argued that the $2.1 billion being spent on the fencing could be put to better use in preventing illegal immigration.

The wall seemed to have some effect on illegal crossings. The number of people held at the border fell 17 percent in 2008. Yet it is estimated that up to two thousand immigrants a day still cross the southwest border.

Other anti-immigrant strategies have been implemented. For example, a new Arizona state law punishes any employer who knowingly hires undocumented workers. Yet as of March 2008, not one employer had been punished for violating this law. While the debate rages on, illegal workers find themselves locked into low-paying jobs with little financial security and few rights to health care and other benefits. Meanwhile, legal Hispanic immigrants wait patiently as nearly 1.5 million applications for visas and naturalization papers slow down the process of citizenship. New 2007 legislation called for a pathway to citizenship for those illegal immigrants if they abided by certain rules. Like earlier anti-immigration bills, it became deadlocked in Congress and has not passed.

Many Hispanic Americans left the demonstrations for the voting booth in November 2008 and they voted in unprecedented numbers. An impressive 67 percent of the Latino vote in the presidencial election went to Democratic winner Barack Obama.

Hispanic voters have a big impact on election results. Here, they vote in the presidential primary of 2008.

THE IMMIGRATION QUESTION

ABAJO
Don't send my job to Mexico
CON NAFTA
NO NAFTA
NOT THIS NAFTA
ABAJO CON NAFTA
TEXAS LCLAA ON THE MARCH!
UAW SAYS...
NO TO NAFTA
UAW SAYS...
NO TO NAFTA
JOBS WITH JUSTICE
LCLAA DICE ABAJO CON NAFTA
Tell Congress
NO NAFTA

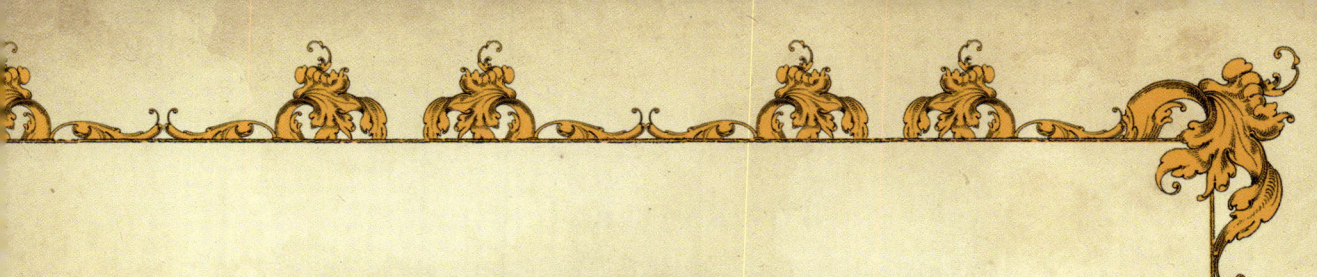

THE NORTH AMERICAN FREE TRADE AGREEMENT

As of 2007, the North American Free Trade Agreement (NAFTA) is the largest trade agreement ever made. The agreement, which went into effect on January 1, 1994, ended most tariffs (trade taxes) among the United States, Canada, and Mexico. Supporters of NAFTA said that increased trade would boost the Mexican economy and give fewer Mexicans reason to immigrate to the United States. At the same time, NAFTA would result in more high-paying jobs for American workers.

Those against NAFTA say it has mostly benefited business owners, not workers. Some American businessmen have moved their operations to Mexico, where labor and operating costs are lower. American employees of these companies have found themselves without jobs. As for the Mexican people, it seems they are no better off than they were before.

The reality falls somewhere in the middle of these two opposing views. It is true that the flood of American goods has hurt Mexican farmers, as food prices have dropped drastically. However, the high poverty rate in Mexico has fallen since NAFTA, and personal incomes are up. Former Mexican president Vicente Fox was encouraged. In 2000 he called for a second phase of NAFTA that would allow people to travel back and forth across the U.S.-Mexico border as easily as goods did. Then the terrorist attacks of September 11, 2001, took place, and Americans rejected any plan to make the border less secure. The debate over NAFTA continues.

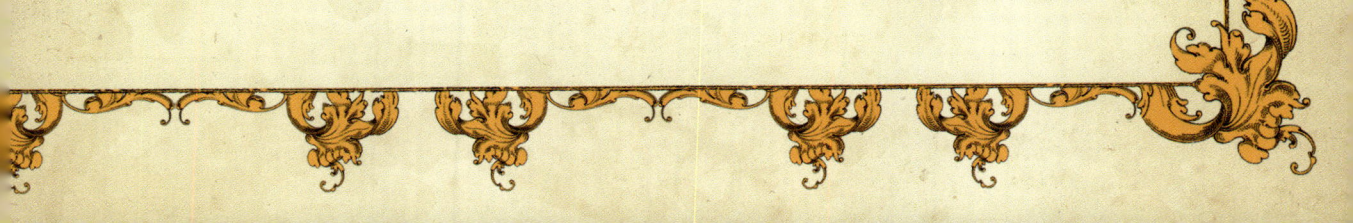

The Rafters of Cuba

While Mexicans and Central Americans have been risking their lives as they cross the treacherous deserts of the American borderlands or the wild waters of the Rio Grande, thousands of Cubans have been taking similar risks. They have tried to reach the United Sates on the high seas.

The largest exodus of Cubans to America since the Mariel Boatlift happened in September 1994, when Cuban dictator Fidel Castro allowed 33,000 of his people to leave. Castro's decision was a highly political one. Two months

Cuban refugees sail on a raft in an attempt to reach the United States.

1990s to 2010

earlier, Cuban government agents had fired on and sunk a tugboat carrying seventy-two Cubans out of Cuba. Forty-one of the men, women, and children drowned as the agents stood by and watched. Castro called the tragedy an accident, but much of the world condemned the action. Since the fall of communism in Eastern Europe a few years earlier, Castro's Cuba had become more and more isolated. Without the powerful support of the Soviet Union, Cuba's economy began to fail. Tighter American trade embargoes on Cuba only worsened the situation.

Castro allowed the 1994 exodus in order to gain himself some goodwill. But his permission did not guarantee that those fleeing the country would arrive safely in the United States. It is estimated that half of the 32,000 immigrants did not survive the ocean journey in unreliable rafts. Those who did survive were held for about a year on American military bases before being allowed into the country. The Cuban American community of Florida helped the new arrivals with jobs and housing, as they had done so many times in the past.

The Elián Gonzalez Affair

The tension between Cuban Americans and Castro's Cuba came to a head over the fate of one unique Cuban refugee. In November 1999, Elián Gonzalez left Cuba with his mother and twelve other refugees. Their 17-foot (5.2-meter) boat drifted aimlessly, and Elián's mother and all but two of the others drowned when the boat capsized before reaching Fort Lauderdale, Florida. Elián was rescued. American officials released him to his American relatives, who took him to their home in Little Havana, in Miami.

Castro demanded that the boy be returned to Cuba and his father, who was divorced from his mother. Elián's father's cousin, Marisleysis Gonzalez, said, "His mother lost her life for him to be here. He needs his freedom and we're his family—he should be with us."

Elián Gonzalez plays baseball at his home in Miami, Florida, in 1999 before he was made to return to Cuba.

The administration of President Bill Clinton, however, saw no way that Elián could stay. Because the boy was a minor, any call for *asylum* would have to be approved by his father, who remained in Cuba. But the Gonzalezes of Miami were not going to give up Elián without a fight. The Cuban American community of Miami rallied around their cause. They held demonstrations, including an emotional candlelit procession that captured headlines around the world. Then Elián's father, Juan Miguel, was allowed to travel to Washington, D.C., where he met with U.S. attorney general Janet Reno. It looked as if the fight to keep Elián in the United States was about to end. But on April 19, 2000, a judge with the eleventh circuit court of appeals in Atlanta, Georgia, ruled that Elián could not be taken out of the country until the full court reviewed the Gonzalezes' motion for asylum.

This ruling was greeted with joy and celebration in Little Havana. Miami's Hispanic American community came together in a moment of solidarity as it never had before. But their victory was short-lived. At about 5 A.M. on April 22, four white vans carrying thirty federal agents drove up to the modest Gonzalez house on New Second Street and twenty-third Avenue. The agents used mace and pepper spray to disperse the small crowd that stood protectively around the house night and day. They broke in the door and found Elián in the arms of a man in a closet. The man was among those who had rescued Elián from the sea six

Elián Gonzalez stands inside a closet with Donato Dalrymple, hiding as federal agents enter the boy's house to take him away.

1990s to 2010

months earlier. The agents carried Elián into a van and took him to Andrews Air Force Base in Maryland, where he was reunited with his father. The pair returned to Cuba two months later.

The Elián Gonzales Affair had an immense impact on Cuban Americans. They felt betrayed by the U.S. government, which they had so faithfully supported in the past. Many non-Hispanic Americans supported Elián's return. The failed efforts of the Cuban Americans seemed to be another sign of their impossible struggle against Castro. But in the decade ahead, as Castro grew older, that struggle would seem less impossible.

Go back
Topic = Snakes
What do they eat?
frogs
holes
Snakes eat frogs.
This is the house that Jack built

CHAPTER FOUR

A Changing Culture

For many years, Spanish language, foods, music, and heritage seemed confined to the Hispanic communities of large cities such as Miami and Los Angeles. That changed drastically at the start of the twenty-first century. Today, Hispanic culture is everywhere—in the media, the arts, food, and fashion. But just as Hispanic culture has transformed mainstream American culture, the culture of the United States has changed Hispanic culture. The cultures are blending in new and often surprising ways.

English or Spanish?—The Bilingual Debate

Language is central to any culture or ethnic group. Many Hispanic immigrants continue to speak their native language—Spanish (or in the case of Brazilians, Portuguese)—in

Opposite: Despite English being their second language, some Hispanic students are spoken to only in English in school.

the United States. Spanish remains the dominant language in many Hispanic communities, especially among first-generation immigrants.

Some Americans see Spanish as a threat to their culture. Organizations such as U.S. English Inc. support making English the official language of the United States. In Southern California, and in other areas with large Hispanic populations, local residents are divided over how bilingual they want their communities to be. They debate whether school materials, street signs, and voter ballots should be written in both English and Spanish. Some Americans believe that all Hispanics should be required to learn and speak English.

But the future of English is not as threatened as some would make it. A 2007 Pew Hispanic Center survey turned up some surprising results. Of the 14,000 Hispanic

This 2000 presidential ballot in Florida was printed in both English and Spanish.

1990s to 2010

50

Americans surveyed, only 23 percent of first-generation adult Hispanics said they could carry on a meaningful conversation in English. But the percentage jumps to 88 percent among second-generation Hispanics and 94 percent among members of the third generation.

Younger Hispanics recognize that in order to be successful in American society at large, it is important to speak English fluently. At the same time, they are proud of their Hispanic heritage and realize that Spanish is part of that heritage. This message is reinforced in the Hispanic media. "Speak English, Live Latino" is the motto of Sí TV, the first English-language cable TV channel for Hispanics.

Tu Ciudad (*Your City*), a magazine for upwardly mobile Hispanics in Los Angeles, was started in 2005. It is the city's first Hispanic magazine written wholly in English. At the same time, its editor-in-chief, Oscar Garza, believes that young Hispanics should not shun Spanish as a "symbol of culture and poverty [they are] trying to escape."

While many Hispanics will continue to speak Spanish, especially in their own communities, many experts believe that English will remain the more important language in the United States—for Hispanics and Anglos alike.

The Media

The mainstream media—especially television and movies—does not yet fully reflect themes and issues important to Hispanic Americans. Hispanic actors and actresses are still struggling to overcome stereotypical roles that cast them as criminals, drug addicts, and prostitutes. However, the Hispanic media is growing, both in English and Spanish, and it serves an audience of millions. Telemundo and Univision, the two largest Hispanic television networks in the United States, offer a wide variety of traditional programming, from game shows to talk shows. Mun2, a new branch of Telemundo begun in 2001, is primarily a music channel for younger viewers. It has expanded into other kinds of programming with youth appeal, including reality shows. In one reality show, called *The Chicos Project*, a Dominican hip-hop artist from New York teams up with a Mexican American neo-punk band from Los Angeles.

Popular Hispanic music such as *reggatone* is a mainstay of Spanish-language radio stations. Hispanic talk shows are also popular and give a voice to Hispanic American communities in many cities. During the demonstrations and walkouts of May 2006 and May 2007, radio hosts played a crucial role in uniting the Hispanic community and urging it to action. Pedro Biaggi, a popular morning host on an FM station, feels that he is serving a forgotten community of Central American immigrants. "Never have we Latinos felt as insecure and persecuted as we do now," Biaggi says. "I'm Puerto Rican . . . I am my audience, and I feel totally committed to helping them."

Equally committed are Hollywood actors such as Cuban American Andy Garcia and Mexican American Salma

Hayek. Both have used their star power to finance and produce documentaries and fiction films that deal with Hispanic history and issues.

In one instance, the American public has embraced a Hispanic program without even knowing it. Most people do not know that the popular ABC series *Ugly Betty* is based on a Colombian *telenovela* about a Latina struggling to succeed in the fashion industry of New York City. The title character is played by Honduran-American actress America Ferrera. The problems that Betty faces are both specific to Hispanics and universal to all people who feel like outsiders.

Cuban American actor Andy Garcia was nominated for an Academy Award as Best Supporting Actor for his role in *The Godfather, Part III* (1990).

Fine Arts

Contemporary Hispanic American artists have used their art to express the hopes and concerns of their people in new and innovative ways. Mexican American muralist Judy Baca completed her 210-foot *mural*, *The World Wall: A Vision of the Future Without Fear*, in 1998. The portable mural shows scenes of peace and cooperation between peoples of different nations. Since its completion, it has been displayed around the world. Working with hundreds of volunteers, Baca helped produce 105 murals in communities around Los Angeles County between 1988 and 2003.

A Changing Culture

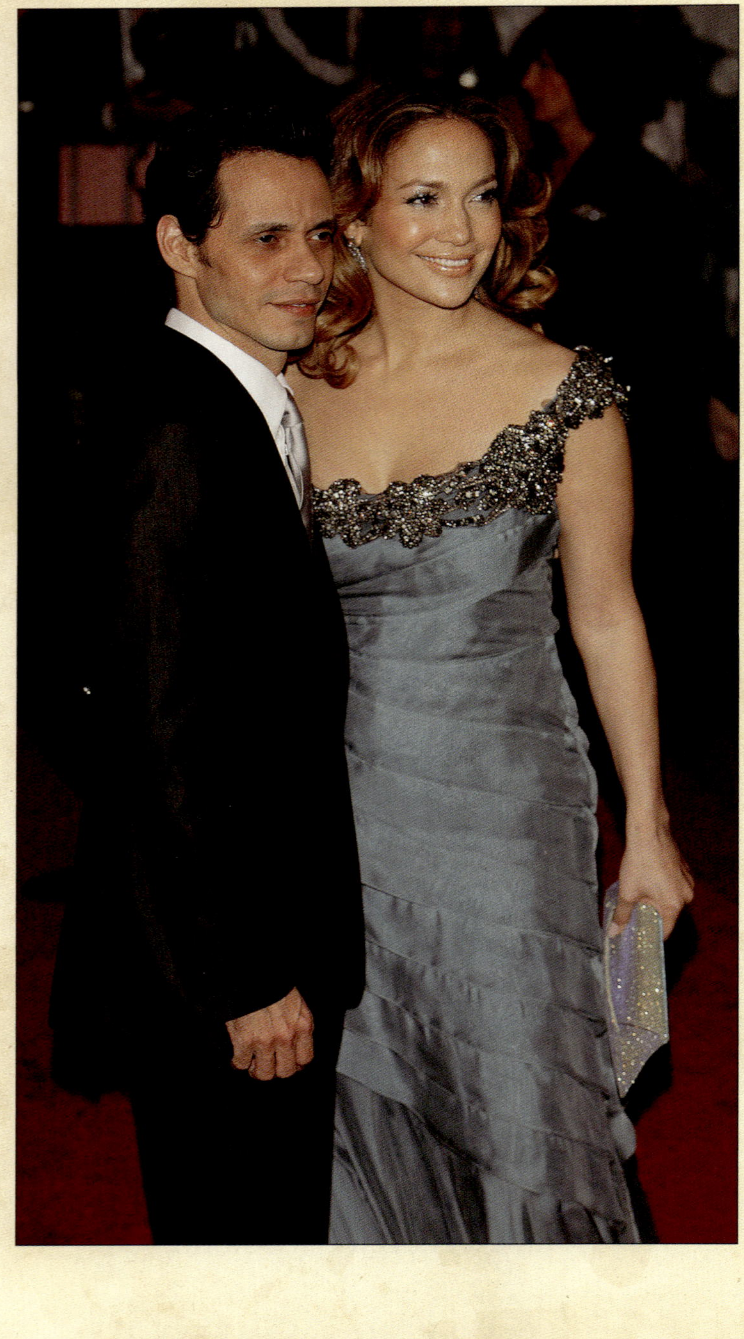

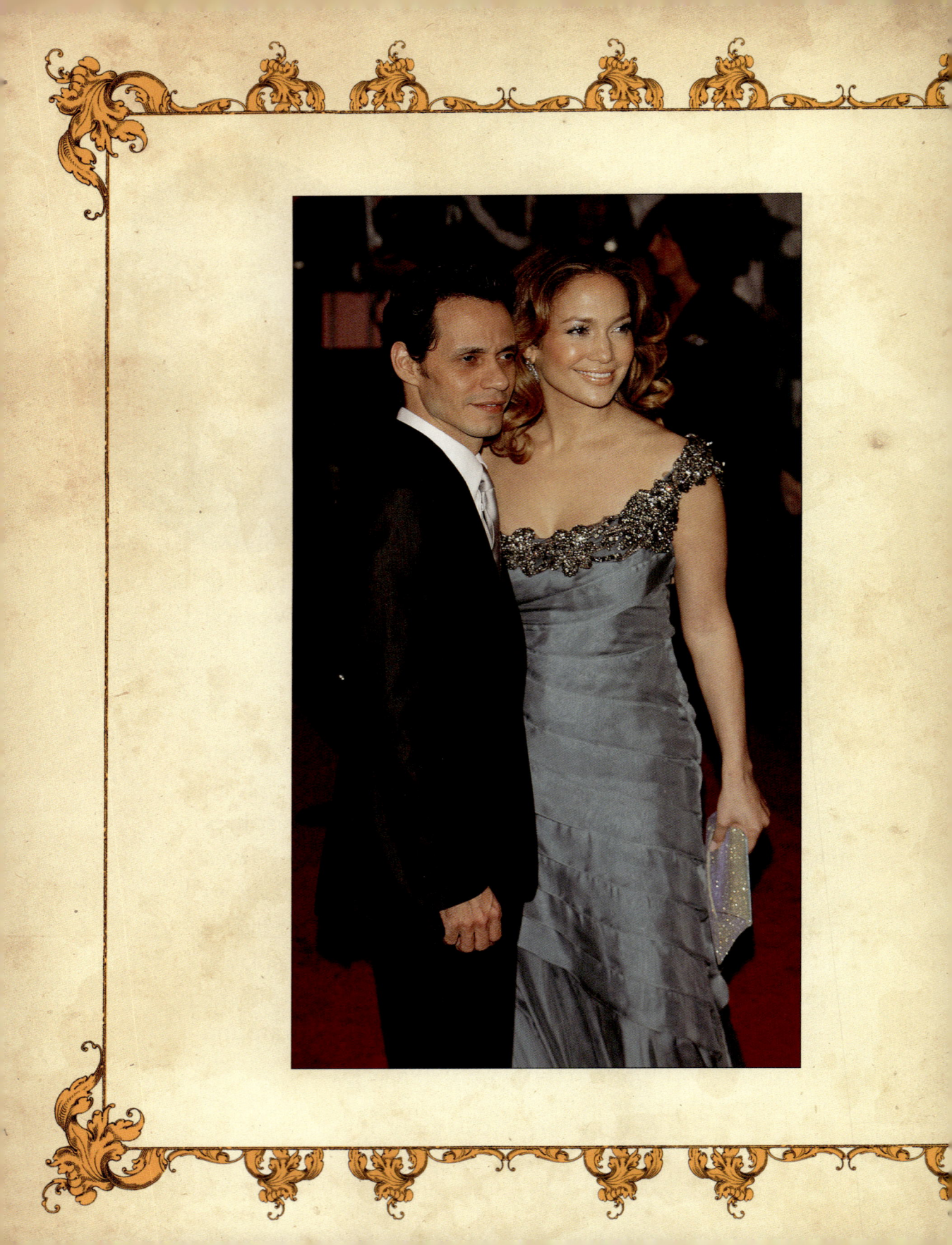

JENNIFER LOPEZ — HISPANIC SUPERSTAR

Few Hispanic entertainers have equaled the success and fame of Jennifer Lopez. Lopez was born into a middle-class Puerto Rican-American family in Bronx, New York, in 1969. Her mother was a kindergarten teacher and her father a computer technician. After high school, Lopez went to college for a semester before quitting to pursue a career as a dancer and actress. Her first big break was getting a job on the hit television comedy series *In Living Color* as one of the infamous Fly Girl dancers. She left the show in 1992 and landed her first major film role three years later in *My Family, Mi Familia* (1995), a saga of three generations of a Mexican-American family in East L.A. Stardom came to Lopez with the leading role in *Selena* (1997), a movie about the life and tragic death of famed *tejena* singer Selena Quintanilla Perez.

Lopez began a successful recording career with the release of her first solo album in 1999. Later, for the movie *The Wedding Planner* (2001), she was paid a salary of nine million dollars, making her the highest-paid Latina actress to date. As good a businesswoman as she is a performer, Lopez has her own production company, puts out a line of perfume and clothing and owns a Cuban restaurant in California. She is married to Puerto Rican American singer Marc Anthony. The couple has twin boys, who were born in February 2008.

The tradition of *santos*, a type of religious folk art, goes back more than two centuries in New Mexico. Contemporary *santeros*, such as Luis Tapia and his son Sergio, have adapted the old tradition to contemporary issues, such as gang violence and alcoholism. For example, in his *Pieta,* modeled after the religious image of Mary holding the body of the dead Jesus, Tapia shows a modern Hispanic mother holding the body of her son, who is a victim of a shooting.

Not all Hispanic artists portray serious themes. Cuban American cartoonist Carlos Castellanos and his writing partner, Hector Cantu, first published their comic strip *Baldo* in 2000. The comic is about the misadventures of a fifteen-year-old Hispanic American boy and his family. It was the first syndicated comic strip about Hispanic Americans by Hispanic Americans.

Religion

As Hispanics went to the United States, they took their religion—Roman Catholicism—with them. Hispanic Americans are among the most devout and emotional of Catholics, but they have not always felt at home with the Catholic Church in their adopted homeland. Many have been uncomfortable with the more traditional, low-keyed style of the U.S. Catholic Church. They have found it difficult to relate to non-Hispanic priests, and they miss hearing Mass in their own language.

Parishioners take part in a Pentecostal service held in New Jersey.

As a result, many Hispanics have left the Catholic Church and have joined Protestant sects, particularly the Pentecostal. According to a February 2008 Pew Forum survey, more than a million Hispanic Catholics have joined *Pentecostal* churches since arriving in the United States. They have been drawn to the church's emotional worship, evangelical slant, and community outreach.

The Catholic Church is anxious to prevent Hispanics from defecting to the Pentecostals. In the past, Hispanics have been faithful and obedient Catholics. They make up about 15 percent of all seminarians studying for the priesthood and brotherhood in the United States. The church is putting more Hispanic, Spanish-speaking priests in churches where the majority of parishioners are Hispanic. Its model is the Spanish

A Changing Culture

It is not uncommon for a number of generations to live together in a Hispanic family.

Apostolate in Brooklyn-Queens, New York. More than fifty Spanish-speaking priests there serve the needs of South American immigrants in greater New York City.

Family Values

Hispanic Americans place a high value on family life. Extended families of uncles, aunts, cousins, and grandparents often live together in one house. Family members who arrive in the United States are given a place to stay and help in finding a job.

In traditional Hispanic cultures, grandparents are to be respected, and women are expected to be obedient. More recent generations of Hispanic women are far more independent than their mothers and grandmothers were, however. Many young people are earning enough money to move out of the barrio and into middle-class suburbs. They are speaking English at work, making new friends outside the Hispanic community, and—at a rate of about one-third—marrying non-Hispanics.

As Hispanic America changes and becomes a more integral part of American society, some people wonder if it can continue to hold on to the best of its traditions and culture.

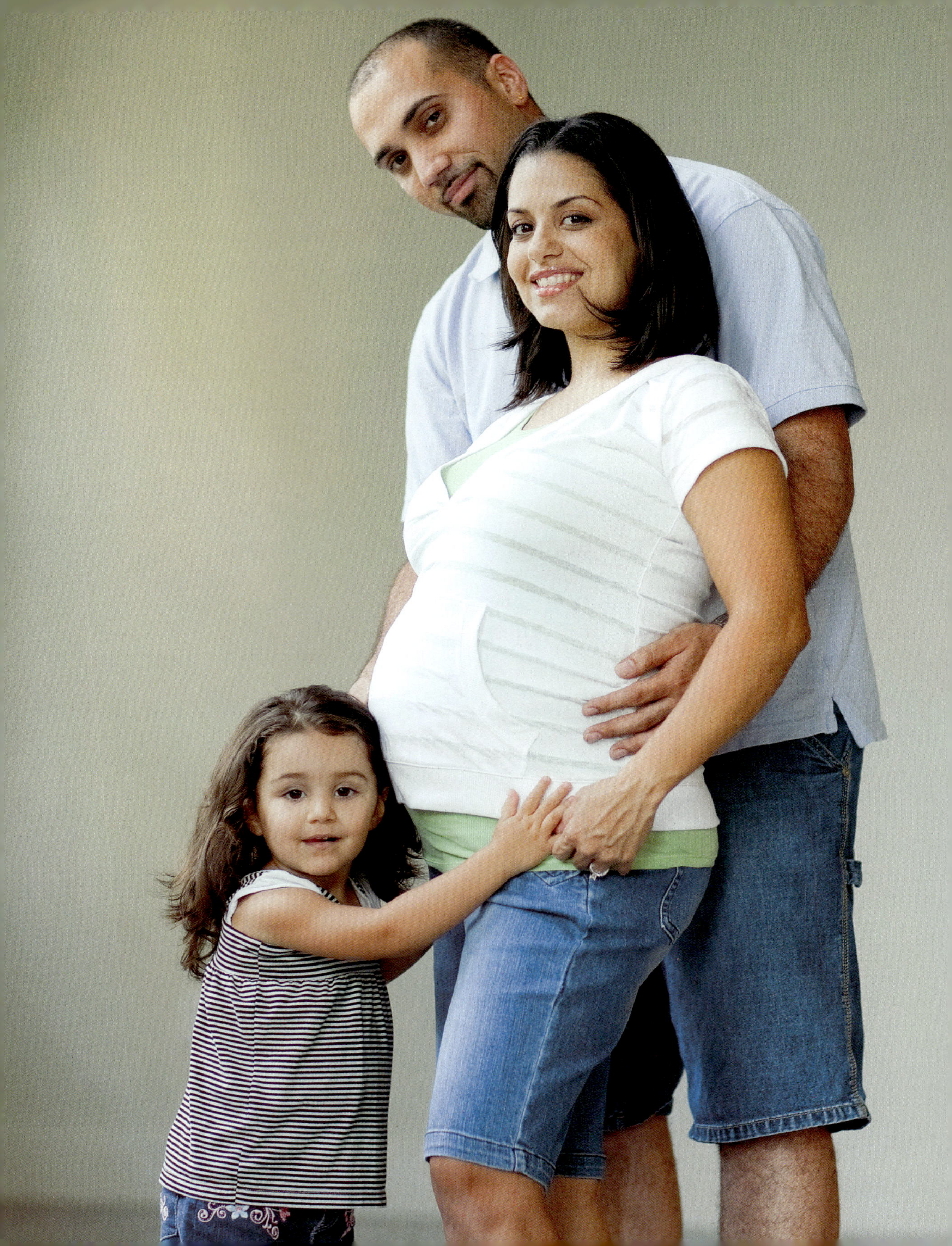

CHAPTER FIVE

Looking to the Future

IN THE YEARS AHEAD, THE NATION'S LARGEST minority is only going to grow larger. By 2050, according to the U.S. Census Bureau, Hispanic Americans will number 133 million. In the half century from 2000 to 2050, the Hispanic population will increase by nearly three times. The reason for this incredible growth is that Hispanics are marrying early and having large families. There are also many more Hispanic Americans of childbearing age than there were in previous years. The median age of Hispanic Americans is 27.4 years, compared to 36.4 years for the U.S. population as a whole.

What will this tremendous growth mean for Hispanic Americans? And what will it mean for all Americans? As non-Hispanic whites become a minority for the first time in modern American history, will they lose their economic and political

Opposite: Many Hispanics in the United States have large families, which contributes to the growing Hispanic population.

power to Hispanics, African Americans, and other growing minorities? Will the United States be a different and more diverse nation?

The answer to this last question is undeniably "yes." The new generation of Hispanics is adapting to mainstream American culture and social ways, while preserving what is unique about its own cultures. This adaptation will accelerate as more Hispanics marry outside their ethnic group—including members of different Hispanic groups as well as non-Hispanics. In 2004, about half of third-generation Hispanics who got married were married to non-Hispanic spouses. Economic and political power will also be key factors in integrating Hispanics into the American mainstream. Let us look at these two important factors in terms of the progress that is being made today and the challenges that lie ahead.

Economics and Education

The last few decades have seen tremendous economic gains for Hispanic Americans. Between 1994 and 2006, the average Hispanic household income increased by 20 percent, from $31,500 a year to $37,800 a year. In that same time period the total number of skilled, blue-collar jobs held by Hispanics more than doubled, from 11 percent to 25 percent. In 1995, about 30 percent of all Hispanic Americans lived below the poverty level. In 2006, this number dropped to about 20 percent.

Many young Hispanics are using education to help them achieve what they want to in their lives.

Much of this economic progress can be attributed to education. Old traditions among Mexican Americans and other Hispanic groups put a higher value on hard work than on education. But these traditions are beginning to break down. Immigrant parents want their children to have better opportunities in the workplace, and they are realizing that education is the answer. High school dropout rates among Hispanics, once as high as half, are falling. About two-thirds of Hispanic youth are now finishing high school, and 25 percent are continuing on to college. Hispanics with some college education or a college degree are moving up the employment ladder to higher-paying jobs and management positions.

LOOKING TO THE FUTURE

The resulting growth in economic power is startling. In 2006, in California alone, there were an estimated 340,000 Hispanic-owned small to medium-size businesses. About 25,000 of them took in more than a million dollars in annual *revenue*. These successes are causing banks—both in the United States and in Latin America—to take notice. They are reaching out to help Hispanic American businesses—a real sign of economic power.

But there are still many challenges ahead. The one-third of Hispanic youth who do not finish high school have few work skills and are mostly stuck in low-paying jobs. The *recession* of 2007 and 2008 resulted in the loss of many jobs in industry and agriculture nationwide. It has left many working-class Hispanics—including many with a high school education—unemployed or underemployed. For the first time in years, millions of Hispanic immigrants have little or no money to send home to their families in their homelands. This sign of economic insecurity hurts the economies of their homelands, which have benefited from millions of dollars sent home from the United States.

With barely enough money to make ends meet, many working-class Hispanic Americans cannot afford health insurance for their families. In a small northeastern state such as Connecticut, 10 percent of the population is Hispanic, but Hispanics comprise 30 percent of the state's uninsured.

A DOMINICAN AMERICAN

Nineteen-year-old Jorge Pesok typifies the spirit of the new generation of Hispanic Americans. He is energetic, ambitious, and very American. Pesok's father was born in Argentina and moved to Israel when he was eleven. His mother is from the Dominican Republic (DR), where his parents met.

Pesok was born in the DR, and he came to the United States with his parents when he was three and a half years old. He has few memories of the land of his birth. "I remember climbing mango trees, and my cousin picking coconuts from trees and splitting them open with a machete," he says.

Pesok's parents are divorced. Until recently, he lived in a largely Dominican neighborhood in Bronx, New York, with his mother, who speaks no English. Pesok joined the U.S. National Guard at age seventeen, and he was trained to be a *paralegal* for the U.S. Army. The National Guard is helping to pay for his college education. Jorge attends the University of Connecticut, where he studies political science and communications. He plans to continue on to law school, to enter politics, and to become a member of the U.S. House of Representatives, in order to help poor and underrepresented people.

Pesok is bilingual, but he speaks Spanish only with his mother, sister, and father. He does not identify strongly with Hispanic Americans. "I like being American," he says, "but I love Hispanic food, especially when my mom cooks it for me."

The Political Scene—Room for Improvement

For all their growing economic clout, Hispanics have lagged in political power for years. In 2002, there were 13 million adult citizens in the Hispanic population, but only about 5 percent voted in elections. As a result, elected officials have been slow to address Hispanic issues and few Hispanics have been elected to office. Prior to the 2008 election, there were only a handful of Hispanics serving in the House of Representatives and only one in the U.S. Senate. Bill Richardson of New Mexico, a presidential contender in 2008, is currently the only Hispanic governor.

This situation will likely change in the future. Hispanics are beginning to realize the importance of acting as a strong *electorate* to get their needs met. The mobilization of millions of Hispanic workers in the job walkouts in 2006 through 2008 showed them their strength in numbers. Social action led many Hispanic citizens to register to vote.

Republican president George W. Bush, a former governor of Texas, was popular with many Hispanics in the presidential elections of 2000 and 2004. But in 2008, however, the anti-immigration views of some Republican candidates and politicians drove many Hispanics back to the Democrats' side, where they previously had stood. A record 78 percent of the Hispanics who voted in the 2008 presidential primaries chose Democratic candidates. The day that Americans will elect a Hispanic American president may not be so far off.

President George W. Bush was popular with a number of Hispanic voters in both of his elections.

LOOKING TO THE FUTURE

The Future of Immigration

Hispanic immigration—both legal and illegal—continues to be strong in the twenty-first century. According to the Citizenship and Immigration Services, in the summer of 2007 there were a record 1.4 million applications for citizenship—a large percentage of them from Hispanics—which was nearly double what they received the year before. This trend has since slowed down.

Visas and naturalization papers will take an average of eighteen months to process until at least 2010. While the United States continues its ongoing debate over illegal immi-

After naturalization papers are processed, immigrants attend a ceremony where they are sworn in as U.S. citizens.

grants, the human tide from the south continues to flow across the southern border despite increased efforts to stem it.

Many Hispanic Americans and non-Hispanic citizens feel that forging a pathway to citizenship for illegal immigrants already residing in the United States is the only practical solution to this problem. As the non-Hispanic white population continues to age in the years ahead, immigrants will fill in the workforce and help keep the American economy moving forward. "It's going to be immigrant labor supporting the aging white population," believes University of California at Los Angeles (UCLA) *sociologist* Edward Telles, quoted in the *Los Angeles Times*. "They need this growing Latino population to maintain the Social Security system."

But some Americans fear immigration must slow down so that the United States will not become overcrowded and unable to meet its citizens' needs. And many sociologists think that the flow past U.S. borders will lessen if conditions in Latin American countries improve. As governments in these countries become more stable and their economies grow, their citizens might have less reason to search for a better life elsewhere. This process is already well under way in countries such as Brazil, Argentina, and Chile. But conditions in other countries, such as Colombia and many nations in Central America, are still politically unstable. The United States can help with this stabilization process by forming stronger Latin American policies and offering more economic aid and support.

Cuba after Castro

Among Latin American countries, Cuba holds a unique position. The communist regime of Fidel Castro has caused the United States to take an aggressive, anti-Cuba stance for nearly five decades. In the hope of weakening Castro, the U.S. government has imposed a string of trade *embargoes* against Cuba. Yet by blaming anti-Cuba policy in the United States for every problem he has faced, Castro has managed to strengthen his position as Cuba's leader.

But the years have taken their toll on the world's longest-reigning head of state. In February 2008, an ill and aging eighty-one-year-old Castro officially relinquished power when he turned over the presidency to his seventy-four-year-old brother, Raul. Raul Castro's promises of reform have brought renewed hope and anticipation to millions of Cuban Americans. Many believe that the end of communism in Cuba is in sight. But what will Cuba after the Castros be like? And how will life change for Cuban Americans?

Again, the United States could help to shape the future of this island nation. As editorial writer Cynthia Tucker has pointed out, Cuba is better "fertile ground for American-style democratic institutions than, say Iraq," where the United States has been waging war since 2005.

While it is unlikely many Cuban Americans will want to return permanently to Cuba, it is equally unlikely that many Cubans in Cuba will feel the need to immigrate to the United States.

Cuban president Raul Castro waves to the crowd during a speech he gave in Cuba in July 2008.

LOOKING TO THE FUTURE

The Pan-Hispanic Movement

Cuban Americans, along with their Mexican and Puerto Rican brothers and sisters, have until now largely dominated Hispanic culture in the United States. That may soon change. Hispanic Americans are recognizing that they can be more effective and powerful if they unite as one. With the spread of Hispanic communications and media, a broadening economic market, and a growing electorate, differences are beginning to fade, and Hispanics are unifying for their mutual benefit. They are working together to solve common problems that face all of them in areas such as education, crime, social welfare, employment, and housing.

In the years to come, Hispanic America will continue to grow and change. It will become more mainstream, while holding on to the best of its culture and traditions. Like previous ethnic and racial minorities before them, from the Irish to African Americans, Hispanic Americans are bringing their talents and energies, their dreams and hopes to their new homeland. That, in the end, can only benefit all Americans.

Timeline

1994 The North American Free Trade Agreement (NAFTA) takes effect in the United States, Canada, and Mexico.

Cuba experiences the largest antigovernment rally since Castro took power.

In September, Castro allows 33,000 Cubans to immigrate to the United States on rafts and boats.

1999 White non-Hispanics become a minority in California, where 47 percent of the population is Hispanic.

2000 Elián Gonzales, Cuban child refugee, is taken from his Miami relatives' home by government agents and eventually is sent back to Cuba with his father.

2002 In November, Bill Richardson is elected the first Hispanic governor of New Mexico.

2003 On January 22, the U.S. Census Bureau announces that Hispanics are the largest minority in the United States, totaling about 37 million; later that year, the bureau announces that there are more Puerto Ricans living on the mainland United States than in Puerto Rico.

2005 In February, President George W. Bush appoints Alberto Gonzales the first Hispanic attorney general.

On February 19, Fidel Castro steps down from power after forty-nine years as Cuba's leader.

On May 1, millions of Hispanic Americans nationwide walk off the job to protest proposed anti-immigration legislation.

In May, Mexican American Antonio Villaraigosa is elected mayor of Los Angeles.

Work begins on a 50-foot-high (15-meter-high), 700-mile-long (1,127-kilometer-long) fence at the U.S.-Mexico border.

2008 On November 4, between 9.6 and 11 million Latino voters cast ballots in the presidential election, a record number.

Glossary

Anglos White Americans not of Hispanic descent.
asylum Shelter or protection granted by a country to refugees from another country.
bilingual Involving or speaking two languages.
commonwealth A nation, state, or other political unit.
communist Following a system of government in which one political party or government controls all property.
Creole A language developed from mixed French or Spanish and black descent, allowing speakers of both languages to communicate with one another.
electorate A body of people entitled to vote in an election.
embargoes Restrictions on trade between one country and another.
felony A serious crime usually punishable by a prison term of more than one year.
first-generation immigrant Describing a person who is born in one country and moves to another.
immigration The act of moving permanently from one country to another.
infrastructure The basic facilities serving a country, city, or region.
mural A large painting created on a wall or other huge space.
paralegal A professional who assists lawyers in their work.
Pentecostal Relating to Christian groups that are conservative in their beliefs and stress a spiritual and emotional link with God.
recession A period of economic decline.
reggatone A popular kind of Hispanic dance music similar to rap.
revenue Income brought in by a business operation.
salsa A Hispanic sauce made from tomatoes, chilies, and other ingredients.
santeros Folk artists who make santos.
santos Religious folk paintings or statues made in the American Southwest or Puerto Rico.
second-generation Describing a person who is born in one country but whose parents came from another country.

sociologist A scientist who studies human society and its workings.
suburbs Communities immediately outside or surrounding a city.
tejana Describing a person who is from Texas and is of Hispanic descent.
telenovelas Popular daytime dramas on Latin American and Hispanic American television networks.
undocumented immigrants People who cross national borders in a way that violates the immigration laws of the destination country.
visa Official paperwork that permits someone to enter a country.

Further Information

Books

Hunter, Miranda. *Latino Americans and Immigration Laws: Crossing the Border* (Hispanic History). Philadelphia: Mason Crest Publishers, 2006.

McIntosh, Kenneth and Marsha. *South America's Immigrants to the United States: The Flight from Turmoil* (Hispanic History). Philadelphia: Mason Crest, Publishers, 2006.

Sanna, Ellyn. *Mexican Americans' Role in the United States: A History of Pride, a Future of Hope* (Hispanic History). Philadelphia: Mason Crest Publishers, 2005.

Seidman, David. *Creating a New Future, 1986 to Present* (Latino-American History). New York: Chelsea House, 2007.

Websites

Famous Latinos and Latinas
http://www.lasculturas.com/lib/libFamosos.php
 Links and information on Hispanic American authors, actors, musicians, and historical figures.

The Smithsonian Latino Center
http://latino.si.edu/
 This site includes information about Radio Latino, New Kids Corner, and Latino Resources.

Bibliography

Davis, Mike. *Magical Urbanism: Latinos Reinvent the US City*. New York: Verso, 2000.

Ramos, Jorge. *The Latino Wave: How Hispanics Will Elect the Next American President*. New York: HarperCollins, 2004.

Suro, Roberto. *Strangers Among Us: How Latino Immigration is Transforming America*. New York: Alfred A. Knopf, 1998.

Index

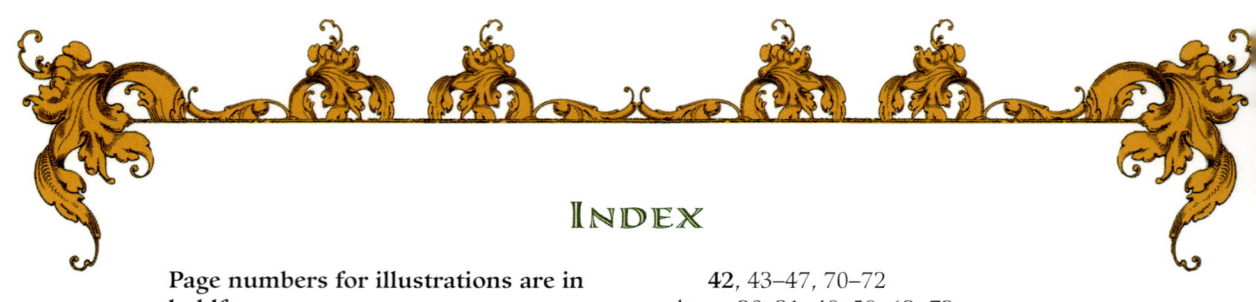

Page numbers for illustrations are in boldface.

African Americans, 4, 6, 9, 25
Alaska, Hispanic Americans in, 8
Anglos. *See* whites
Anthony, Marc, 30, **54**, 55
Argentina, 22, 69
Arizona, illegal immigrants in, 38
art/artists, 53, 56

Baca, Judy, 53
Baird, Zoe, 35
Baldo (comic strip), 56
ballot, bilingual, **50**
Biaggi, Pedro, 52
boatlifts, 15, **42**, 42–43
border crossings, 11–12, **12**, 35, 36–38, 41, 42–43, 69
Border Protection, Anti-terrorism and Illegal Immigration Control Act of 2005, 33–34
Brazil, 14, 22, 69
Bush, George W., 66, **67**

California, Hispanic Americans in, 6, 8, 23–28, 51, 64
Cantu, Hector, 56
Caribbean Islands, **7**, 17, 22
Carnaval Miami, **18**, 21
Castellanos, Carlos, 56
Castro, Fidel, 15, **16**, 17, 20, 23, 42–43, 44, 47, 70
Castro, Raul, 70, **71**
Catholic Church, 56–58
Central America, 6, 7, 14, 17, 24, 42, 69
Chicos Project, The (TV series), 52
children, 9, 35, **48**
Chile, 22, 69
citizenship, 8, 35, 36, 39, **68**, 68–69
Colombia, 22, 69
communism, 15, 17, 23, 43, 70
crime, 24–25, 72
Cuban Americans, 15–17, **18**, 19–23, **20**, **42**, 43–47, 70–72
culture, 20–21, 49–59, 62, 72

Dalrymple, Donato, **46**
Democratic Party, 39, 66
discrimination, 9, 38
Dominican Americans, 17, 22, 31, 65

East Harlem (New York City), **29**, 31
economics, 62–64, 72
education, 9, 15, **48**, 62–63, **63**
El Salvador, immigrants from, 17, 24
English (language), 9, 19, 21, 49–51, 59

families, **58**, 58–59, **60**, 61
Ferrera, America, 53
festivals, **18**, 21, **30**, 30
Florida, Hispanic Americans in, 14, **18**, 19–23, 25, 43–47
food, 10, 11
French (language), 6, 14

gangs, 25, 56
Garcia, Andy, 52, **53**
Golden Exile generation (Cuban Americans), 20
Gonzalez, Elián, 43–47, **44**, **46**
Great Migration (Puerto Rican Americans), 28
Guatemala, immigrants from, 17
Guevara, Che, **24**

Haitian Americans, **21**, 21
Hayek, Salma, 53
Hispanic Americans, **4**, 5–6, 8–11, 17
   see also Cuban Americans; Mexican Americans; Puerto Rican Americans
Honduras, immigrants from, 22
housing, 8, 72

Illinois, Hispanic Americans in, 8
immigrants, 5, **8**, 10–11, 24, 50–51, 66, 68–69
   illegal, 11–12, 33–39, 42–47, 68–69
   legislation regarding, 33–34, 38, 39, 66

1990s to 2010

78

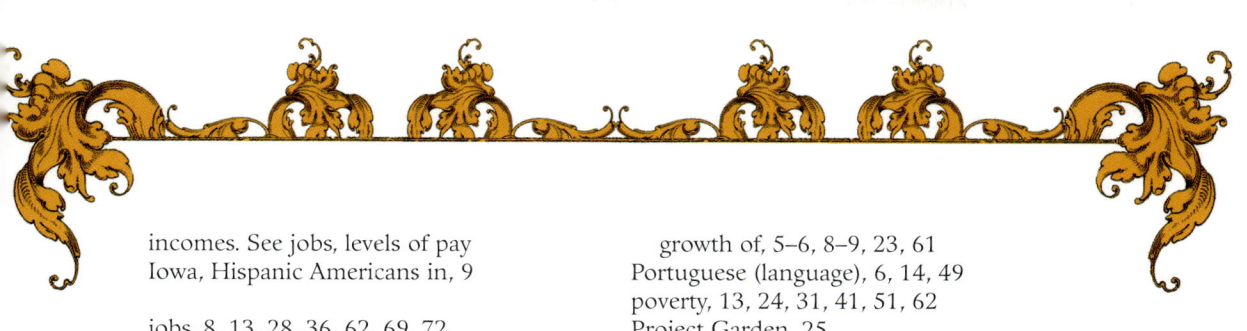

incomes. See jobs, levels of pay
Iowa, Hispanic Americans in, 9

jobs, 8, 13, 28, 36, 62, 69, 72
    levels of pay, 9, 12, 15, 38, 41, 63, 64

Krochmal, Robert, 25

languages, 49–51
    see also English (language); French (language); Spanish (language)
Latin America, 6, **7**, 14, 17, 69
Ligarde, Sebastian, **22**
Little Haiti (Miami), **21**, 21
Little Havana (Miami), 19–21, **20**
Lopez, Jennifer, **54**, 55
Los Angeles, Hispanic Americans in, 23–28, **24**, 51

Maine, Hispanic Americans in, 8
map, **7**
Martin, Ricky, 30
Martinez, Mel, 23
media, 51–53, 72
    see also radio; television
Mexican Americans, 6, **8**, 11–12, **13**, 17, 24–27, 42, 72
Mexico, **7**, 14, 22, 41
Miami, Florida, Hispanic Americans in, **18**, 19–23, 25, 43–47
movies, 22, 51, 53
music, 52

New York City, Hispanic Americans in, 6, 8, 25, 28–31, **29**, 58
Nicaragua, immigrants from, 17, 22
North American Free Trade Agreement (NAFTA), **40**, 40–41
Nuyoricans, 28–31

Obama, Barack, 39
Pan-Hispanic Movement, 72
Pentecostal Church, **57**, 57
Pesok, Jorge, 65
politics, 9–10, 17, 22–23, 26–27, 31, 66–67
population, 11, 13, 15, 19, 24, 66

    growth of, 5–6, 8–9, 23, 61
Portuguese (language), 6, 14, 49
poverty, 13, 24, 31, 41, 51, 62
Project Garden, 25
protests, **32**, 33, 34, **40**, 52, 66
Puerto Rican Americans, 12–15, 17, 22, 28–31, **29**, **30**, 52, 72

radio, 10, 52
Reagan, Ronald, 23
religion, 56–58
Republican Party, 17, 23, 66
Richardson, Bill, **10**, 10, 66
Rivera, Dennis, 30
Rubio, Marco, 23
rural areas, Hispanic Americans in, 9

September 11, 2001, attacks, 35, 41
South America, 6, **7**, 14, 17, 22, 24, 31
Spain, immigrants from, 17
Spanish (language), 6, 9, 14, 19, 21, 49–51, 65
    television programs in, 22, 25, 28
suburbs, Hispanic Americans in, 8

Tapia, Luis, 56
Telemundo (TV network), 28, 52
telenovelas, 22, 53
television, 10, 22, 25, 28, 51–53
Texas, Hispanic Americans in, 6, 8
Texas Border Coalition, 38
Tu Ciudad (*Your City*, magazine), 51

Ugly Betty (TV series), 53
Univision (TV network), 28, 52
Uruguay, immigrants from, 22
U.S. English Inc., 50
Varoni, Miguel, **22**
Velazquez, Nydia, **31**, 31
Villaraigosa, Antonio, 25, **26**, 26–27
voting, 9–10, 14, **39**, 39, **50**, 66

wall, U.S.-Mexican border, 36–38, **37**
West Indies, 6, 14
whites, 6, 9, 23, 61, 69
Wilson, Pete, **35**, 35

INDEX
79

About the Author

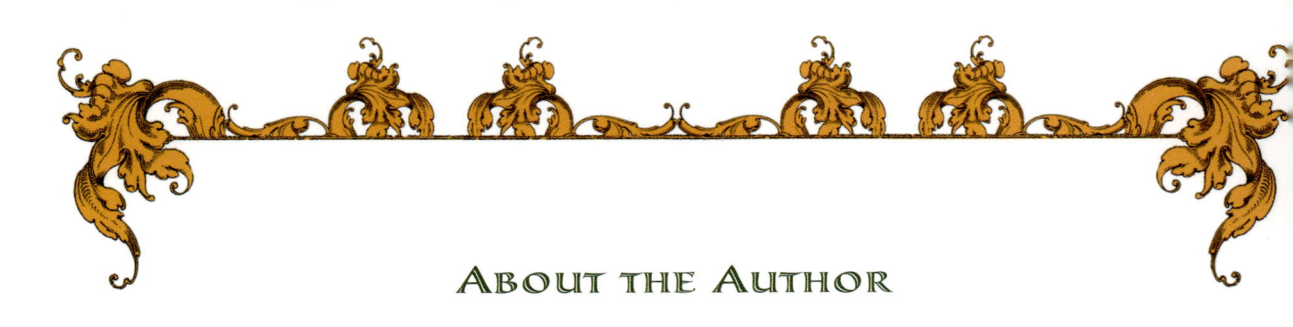

STEVEN OTFINOSKI has written *The New Republic* in Marshall Cavendish's Hispanic America series. He is also the author of *Francisco Coronado: In Search of the Seven Cities of Gold,* *Vasco Nunez de Balboa: Explorer of the Pacific,* and *Ponce de Leon: Discoverer of Florida* in Marshall Cavendish's Great Explorations series.

+
305.8 O

Otfinoski, Steven.
1990s to 2010
Central Kids CIRC - 4th fl

DISCARD

12/09